FLASH POINTS

DISASTER!
TRAGEDIES THAT GRIPPED THE WORLD

Eleanor Cardell

full tilt PRESS

Disaster!
Flash Points

Full Tilt Press
42982 Osgood Road
Fremont, CA 94539
readfulltilt.com

Full Tilt Press publications may be purchased for educational, business, or sales promotional use.

Design and layout by Sara Radka
Copyedited by Renae Gilles

Alamy, 35; Getty Images: 123foto, cover and background, EyeEm, 6, iStockphoto, 48, U.S. Coast Guard, 42; Newscom: akg-images, 15, Courtesy Everett Collection, 5, 7, 19, EPA, 25, 29, 30, 32, Itar-Tass Photos, 31, Jeff Schultz, 42, 43, MCT, 39, 40, Picture History, 7, picture-alliance / Judaica-Samml, 23, REPIK/ ZUFAROV/UKRINFORM/SIPA, 27, UPI, 11, ZUMAPRESS/Earl S. Cryer, 37, ZUMAPRESS/Gary Braasch, 38; Shutterstock: donvictoria, 37, Everett Historical, 18, 20, 21, 22, 23, Gail Johnson, 36, Gwoeli, 17, InnervisionArt, 37, Liukov, 28, Natalia Bratslavsky, 41, Parsadanov, 6, PhilipYb Studio, 7, Praisaeng, 27, Sergey Kamshylin, 26, sondem, 16, SvedOliver, 27, vladlemm, 32, Volodymyr Baleha, 17; Wikimedia, 9 12, Bain News Service, 10, 12, Nationaal Archief, 16, US National Archives & Records Administration, 13

ISBN: 978-1-62920-605-9 (library binding)
ISBN: 978-1-62920-617-2 (eBook)

Contents

THE TRIANGLE FACTORY FIRE

March 25, 1911

At the Triangle **Shirtwaist** Factory in New York City, workers sit bent over tables. They've been sewing for hours. It's almost time to leave. Suddenly, the ninth-floor workers smell smoke. A fire that started on the eighth floor has reached them.

People run for the exits. The narrow hallway to the elevator is packed with workers. The elevator can't hold many people. Fire soon fills the hallway, blocking the exit. People climb onto the fire escape. It crumples beneath their weight and falls to the sidewalk. The fire department arrives, but their ladders are too short. They can't reach the ninth floor. Workers jump from the windows, trying to escape the blaze.

That day, 146 people died. Most of them were young **immigrant** women. It was the deadliest fire in New York City history.

shirtwaist: a type of button-down shirt for women, popular in the early 1900s

immigrant: someone who moves to a new country

In the early 1900s, most of the clothes in the United States were made in New York City. More than 80,000 people worked in clothing factories like the Triangle Shirtwaist Factory.

How and Why

Accidents and disasters often have more than one cause. Many different things come together to cause events that can greatly impact the future. Take a moment to explore some of the things that led to the Triangle factory fire.

Smoking Kills

It was against the rules to smoke inside the factory. But many people did it anyway. A cigarette, or a match used to light a cigarette, is probably what started the Triangle factory fire. It might have been dropped into a bin filled with scraps of cloth. The small fire then consumed the whole building, which was filled with more cloth that caught fire easily.

Laws Did Not Apply

New York had state laws for the construction of buildings. Large buildings needed extra staircases on each floor, and they had to be built with stone floors and metal window frames. But the Triangle factory building was small enough, by only one story, that these laws did not apply.

Not to Code

The Triangle factory building did not meet safety requirements, or codes. The law said that factory exit doors should open outward, but the Triangle factory's doors did not. Doors were not supposed to be locked. However, the factory owners locked them to keep workers inside, and to prevent them from stealing things.

No Warning

The ninth floor didn't have a phone, so no one was able to call and warn the ninth-floor workers about the fire. They didn't realize anything was wrong until the room filled with smoke. By then, it was already too late for many of them to escape.

Unprepared

In the early 1900s, there were many fires in New York City. Firefighters become more efficient. They had better hoses. They responded faster. Firefighters arrived at the Triangle factory very quickly, but they still weren't prepared. Their equipment could only reach up to seven stories.

What Happened Next

The New York City **morgue** wasn't very big. It couldn't hold all the bodies from the Trangle fire. A temporary morgue was built on East 26th Street. The bodies were moved there, instead. Families went there to find their relatives. Some bodies were burned very badly. Even their families couldn't recognize them.

The people of New York City were horrified. How could something like this happen? A women's work **union** called for action. They wanted to **reform** the factories. They worked with the local newspapers. They collected information about bad working conditions.

People held a big meeting. Lots of workers came. There they created the Citizen's Committee for Public Safety. They came up with ideas about how to change the laws. These changes would make factories safer for workers.

New York City paid for a study of factories all over the state. They visited factories and talked to hundreds of workers about the dangerous working conditions. Workers were injured by unsafe machines. They got sick from working with toxic chemicals. Many workers' stories helped create new laws. These laws made factories and workers safer. These laws still exist today.

morgue: a place where bodies are kept until they are identified and buried

union: a group of workers who work to protect their rights in the workplace

reform: to make changes so that something is better

Thousands of people visited the temporary morgue to identify loved ones who had died in the Triangle factory fire.

Employees at the Triangle Shirtwaist Factory were paid about 15 cents an hour. That would be $3.75 today. Since 2009, US law requires workers to be paid at least $7.25 an hour.

Ripple Effects

A single event, no matter how big or small it may seem at the time, can have a big impact on the future. The Triangle factory fire had many far-reaching effects.

Fire Code

A few months after the Triangle factory fire, a law called the Sullivan-Hoey Fire Prevention Law was put into place. This law created the Bureau of Fire Prevention, which is in charge of fire codes. It also conducts fire inspections. The Bureau of Fire Prevention makes sure that workers are safe and can escape if there is a fire.

Worker Safety

In the years after the Triangle factory fire, more than 30 new laws were passed. These laws told owners how to keep workers safe. All doors had to open toward the outside. Large companies had to put in sprinklers and fire extinguishers. Workers had to learn to use a fire extinguisher. Factories became much safer.

Big Changes

In 1912, about 20,000 workers died from workplace accidents across the country. But New York's new safety laws soon spread across the United States. By 2016, the number of yearly deaths had dropped to 4,500.

Workers' Rights

The Triangle factory fire also drew attention to workers' rights. A new law was created in 1912 so women couldn't work more than 54 hours a week. The Fair Labor Standards Act of 1938 made it so most people could only work 40 hours a week. Beyond that, employers have to pay workers extra money, called overtime. This act is still in use today.

DID YOU KNOW?

Every year on March 25, there is a ceremony held in New York City to remember the Triangle factory fire and all those who died in it.

On April 5, 1911, the International Ladies' Garment Workers Union held a funeral march for those lost in the Triangle factory fire.

FRANCES PERKINS

Many people watched the Triangle factory burn that day. One of them was a woman named Frances Perkins. She had come to New York City in 1909. She was working to improve the lives of poor and working people. Seeing the Triangle factory fire inspired her to work even harder. She went into politics, which was very rare for women to do at that time. In 1933, Frances Perkins became the secretary of labor. She worked for President Franklin D. Roosevelt. She was the first woman to serve in the US Cabinet, a part of the government for high-ranking officials.

The Legacy of Tragedy

The Triangle factory fire only burned for half an hour. In that time, almost 50 workers were killed in the fire. One hundred more died trying to escape, by jumping into the elevator shaft or to the sidewalk.

The fire drew the attention of the entire city of New York. Suddenly, people realized how bad the working conditions were. Workers, politicians, and employers worked together. The changes they made to fire codes and workers' rights are still around today, more than 100 years later. But people today still fight for better wages. In 2016, there were protests across the country to raise the minimum wage from $7.25 to $15 an hour.

Factory fires are now very rare in the United States. But they continue to be a problem in other countries. In 2012, more than 300 people died in a clothing factory in Pakistan. That same year, 112 people died in a similar factory in Bangladesh. The workers in these countries are still fighting for their safety and rights.

THE HINDENBURG

May 6, 1937

The German airship *Hindenburg* is about to land in Lakehurst, New Jersey. After 63 trips, this is the first time the airship has crossed the Atlantic Ocean that year. Hundreds of people have gathered for its arrival. The crowd waits for the airship, which was delayed by storms over Lakehurst. Finally, the silver rounded nose of the airship peeks over the treetops. It drifts in slowly before dropping lines, which the ground crew hurries to pick up.

As the airship is towed toward its **mooring**, flames suddenly erupt from the back of the ship. Members of the ground crew begin to run as the orange flame quickly turns to black smoke. Then, there is a series of explosions. Within 40 seconds, the entire airship is on fire. It comes crashing to the ground.

One member of the ground crew and 35 passengers die, witnessed by friends and family in the crowd. This is the end of airship travel.

mooring: a place where a boat or ship is tied up

The *Hindenburg* was 804 feet (245 meters) long, which is longer than two football fields.

How and Why

Accidents and disasters often have more than one cause. Many different things come together to cause events that can greatly impact the future. Take a moment to explore some of the things that led to the *Hindenburg's* fiery crash.

Bad Weather

That day, the weather over Lakehurst was bad. There had been several storms. The captain had been told that he couldn't land until the weather improved. He waited for several hours. Eventually the storms began to clear. The captain was told it was okay to land.

Traveling in Luxury

Traveling on an airship was popular. It was also a luxury. The *Hindenburg* had a fancy dining room, live piano music, and comfortable cabins. It was twice as fast, and twice as expensive, as traveling on a ship at sea.

Flammable Gas

The large "balloon" on top of the airship was filled with gas. This helped it stay in the sky. The *Hindenburg*'s tank was built to be filled with helium, which does not burn. The United States was the world's top manufacturer of helium. But they wouldn't sell it to other countries. They were afraid it would be used to make weapons. Instead, the Germans filled the *Hindenburg*'s tank with hydrogen. Hydrogen catches fire very easily and burns fast.

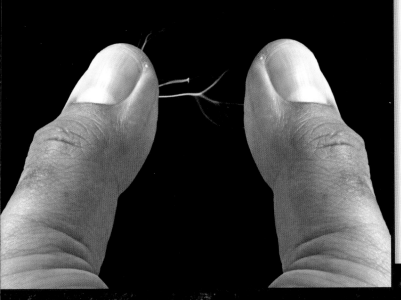

Static Electricity

Nobody knows for sure what actually started the fire. There was a hydrogen leak at the back of the ship. Any small spark could have started the fire. Many experts think it was static electricity. A spark from the static could have lit the gas on fire and destroyed the ship.

What Happened Next

One of the people who watched the *Hindenburg*'s crash was reporter Herbert Morrison. Morrison was recording a news segment. The radio planned to play it later in Chicago. His news report quickly turned to horror as he watched the airship burn. "Oh the humanity!" he cried. Later, people laid those words over **newsreel** films of the ship crashing and burning. This recording is now very well-known.

There were 97 people on board the *Hindenburg*. A total of 36 people died because of the crash. Twenty-six of them died during the crash or in the fire. Another 10 died in the next few days from their injuries. But most of the passengers and crew survived.

The video of the *Hindenburg*'s crash was played all over the world. It was the first public broadcast that went around the globe. Everybody could see the dramatic film of the huge ship on fire. People were shocked and upset. They lost faith in airships. Airships seemed scary and dangerous.

In 1935, the *Hindenburg* flew between Germany and the United States 10 times. In that time, it carried more than 1,000 passengers.

newsreel: a short video about news or current affairs

The *Hindenburg* was also carrying about 17,000 pieces of mail when it crashed. Of those, 176 were recovered.

Ripple Effects

A single event, no matter how big or small it may seem at the time, can have a big impact on the future. The *Hindenburg*'s crash had many far-reaching effects.

Nazi Airship Destroyed

The *Hindenburg* was a German-made airship. It was owned and operated by the Nazi Party, the political group in charge of Germany at the time. Its loss was a blow to the Nazi Party. It was also a national embarrassment for Germany.

Public Disaster

The *Hindenburg* crash was not the most deadly airship accident. However, it was different from the others in one important way. The *Hindenburg*'s destruction was very public. Everyone saw the video, and afterward, the production of airships stopped.

End of an Era

Now, there are almost 24,000 airplane flights in the United States every day. That adds up to 90 million passengers every year. There are a few airships in existence today, but they are no longer used to carry passengers.

Change to Planes

Airplane technology was advanced during World War II (1939–1945). During that time, the United States made more than 50,000 airplanes a year for the war. In 1958, the first official passenger jet carried 180 passengers. It traveled at 550 miles per hour (885 kilometers per hour).

DID YOU KNOW?

Before its crash, the *Hindenburg* was part of the opening ceremony at the 1936 Summer Olympics.

The Legacy of Tragedy

At the time of the *Hindenburg* disaster, airships were one of the fastest ways to travel. They were also comfortable. Many people had dreamed of airship fleets traveling the globe. These dreams were destroyed with the *Hindenburg*. After it crashed, airships no longer carried passengers. By the end of World War II, they had almost disappeared.

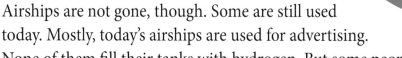

Airships are not gone, though. Some are still used today. Mostly, today's airships are used for advertising. None of them fill their tanks with hydrogen. But some people hope to bring airships back. A few companies are still making airships. Others have plans to build and sell airships. Most of these would not carry passengers. They would be used to transport cargo. Others would be used by the military.

Before the *Hindenburg*, there had been many airship crashes. But none were seen by so many people. It was very upsetting for them to see, and led to the decline of airship travel. But with the spread of television and the internet, people have gotten used to seeing pictures and videos of disastrous events. Now, people see tragedy almost every time they turn on the news.

fleet: a group of ships traveling together

Today, people can tour the site of the *Hindenburg*'s crash. The nearby Navy base even has a small museum, with pieces of the *Hindenburg* on display.

MOST DEADLY

The most deadly airship disaster happened in 1933. The US ship *Akron* crashed on April 4. It was an aircraft carrier. It was also used by the Navy as a scout. It crashed during a storm off the coast of New Jersey. It is believed that the captain of the *Akron* was flying too low. When he tried to go higher, the tail of his airship hit the water. The ship had no lifejackets on board. There was only one rubber raft. There were 76 people on the *Akron*, and 73 died.

DID YOU KNOW?

A special lightweight piano was made for the *Hindenburg*. It was not on board when the airship crashed.

CHERNOBYL

April 26, 1986

It's early morning. Everything is quiet at the Chernobyl Nuclear Power Plant in the former Soviet Union (USSR). The workers are running some tests on the **reactors**. They are going to shut one down for maintenance. This is normal. They have done it before.

Suddenly, the ground is rocked by a powerful explosion. A couple of seconds later, there's another explosion. This one is even even bigger. A nuclear reactor at the plant has just exploded. The power plant is releasing poisonous **radiation** into the air. Multiple buildings are on fire.

Local firefighters respond quickly. Most fires are put out easily in the first 24 hours. But it is another 10 days before the accident is fully contained.

reactor: the part of a nuclear power plant where nuclear reactions happen

radiation: a by-product of nuclear reactions; it is too small to be seen, but is very dangerous

Chernobyl began operating in 1977. Then, it only had one reactor. The next three were built between 1977 and 1983.

An artificial lake was built near the Chernobyl Nuclear Power Plant. The plant used the water to cool the reactors.

Unscheduled Tests

The workers were preparing to shut down one of the reactors. They needed to do some normal maintenance, and had already planned to shut down Reactor 4. They decided to do some tests, as well. These tests would tell them what would happen if the plant lost power.

Lack of Communication

The test team didn't tell anyone what they were doing. The safety team thought they were going to shut down the reactor. Instead, the workers started their tests. Because of this, no one followed the correct safety rules. No one realized that the reactor core was having problems until it was too late.

Unsafe Design

The power plant was not designed in a safe way. There was a power surge. The nuclear fuel became very hot. There was water in the core. The water was supposed to cool the fuel down. But the water turned into steam instead. Pressure built up inside the reactor. The explosion blew the top off the reactor.

Hydrogen Buildup

Scientists don't know for sure why there was a second explosion. Many guess that hydrogen gas built up in the reactor. The hydrogen was lit on fire. This caused another, larger explosion.

What Happened Next?

After the explosion, the reactor started to release radiation into the air. There was also a lot of radioactive **debris**. Some of the debris was heavy and fell close to the reactor. But some was very light. The wind could carry it a long way. This light debris spread across the USSR. It even went into Europe.

The USSR acted quickly. They wanted to stop as much damage as possible. They dumped radiation **absorbents** into the reactor. These helped to lower the radiation. Reactor 4 was also covered in a large concrete dome. This helped stop the radiation from leaking out.

More than 100,000 people who lived close to the power plant were forced to leave. But the radiation had spread even farther than that. More than four million people lived in the area affected by radiation. By the end of the summer, almost 30 people had died. The radiation had poisoned them. Six of these people were firemen. They had helped to put out the fires at the reactor.

The radiation also affected the wildlife. All of the trees in four square miles (10 square kilometers) around Chernobyl died. The dead pine trees all turned a red-brown color. Because of this, the area is called the Red Forest.

debris: scattered pieces of waste

absorbent: a material that is used to soak up something else

When the towns near Chernobyl were evacuated, many people had to leave behind almost everything they owned.

DID YOU KNOW?
At the time of the Chernobyl power plant explosion, two more reactors were being built nearby. These were never completed.

Ripple Effects

A single event, no matter how big or small it may seem at the time, can have a big impact on the future. The disaster at Chernobyl had many far-reaching effects.

Radiation

Radiation can make people sick in many ways. One of these is cancer. After the disaster at Chernobyl, a lot of people were afraid. They thought more people would get cancer. That didn't happen. However, many people still feared that the radiation there would cause cancer.

Nuclear Fear

Lots of countries had nuclear reactors. After Chernobyl, governments made safety rules stronger. But the people still feared nuclear power. They wanted the plants shut down. Since then, Europe has closed about 25 percent of its nuclear power plants.

Preserve

The Exclusion Zone is like a wildlife preserve. Because people aren't allowed inside, there are lots of animals. Some endangered animals live there, too. Scientists think that while some do get sick, the animals are still doing well because they are safe from humans.

Exclusion Zone

The area around Chernobyl is called the "Exclusion Zone." This area is a circle covering about 1,000 square miles (2,600 square kilometers). There is a fence around it to keep people out. Scientists say that it will be about 3,000 years until all the radiation is gone.

DID YOU KNOW?

A breed of wild horse known as Przewalski's horse was almost extinct. In 1998, it was brought to Chernobyl. Today there is a whole herd living in the Exclusion Zone.

Today, people can take tours of the Exclusion Zone for the day and even stay overnight. Guides closely monitor radioactivity levels and only take people to certain areas.

ILLEGAL LIVING

It is illegal to live in the Exclusion Zone. However, about 200 people still live there anyway. Most of them are older people. They grew up there and returned soon after the accident. Now they grow their own food. They call themselves "self-settlers." Some areas don't have dangerous levels of radiation anymore. However, there is still radiation in the plants and animals the self-settlers eat. Scientists think this type of radiation is very bad for young children. The older people living in the Exclusion Zone have a much smaller risk of getting cancer.

The Legacy of Tragedy

The Chernobyl disaster was the worst nuclear disaster in history. More than 77 square miles (200 square kilometers) are covered in radiation. Scientists say the land won't be safe for thousands of years. But the USSR didn't shut down the Chernobyl Nuclear Power Plant. It kept working for 14 years. Chernobyl closed in 2000.

We learned a lot about radiation from the Chernobyl disaster. Scientists are still doing tests. They look at animals, plants, dirt, air, and water. They want to know what radiation does to the environment. Then they will know what to do if there is another nuclear disaster.

Many people thought that everything would die. But that's not what is happening. Animals and plants are still living in the area. However, they still have a lot of radiation in their bodies.

People are still working on cleaning up Chernobyl. In 2016, a steel and concrete building was built over the reactor. It is as big as an Egyptian pyramid and cost $1.7 billion. It blocks radiation so the reactor can be taken apart inside, one piece at a time.

DID YOU KNOW?

In 2016, a huge steel cover was moved into place over Chernobyl's Reactor 4. It is supposed to contain the radiation for 100 years.

THE EXXON VALDEZ OIL SPILL

March 24, 1989

It is just past midnight. The oil tanker *Exxon Valdez* is leaving Prince William Sound, in Alaska. It is on its way to Long Beach, California. The night is calm and still.

Suddenly, its **hull** rams up against underwater rocks. The ship has 11 fuel cells. Eight of them tear open. Oil begins spilling into the sea. The **currents** carry it through the water. More than 1,000 miles (1,600 kilometers) of coastline will soon be covered in oil. The oil poisons the water. Thousands of animals die. Many **ecosystems** are destroyed.

Official reports guess that 11 million gallons (42 million liters) of oil were spilled. Some people say that this guess is too low. At the time, it was the largest oil spill in US waters.

hull: the body of a ship

current: water that moves in one direction

ecosystem: a specific environment and the animals and plants that live there

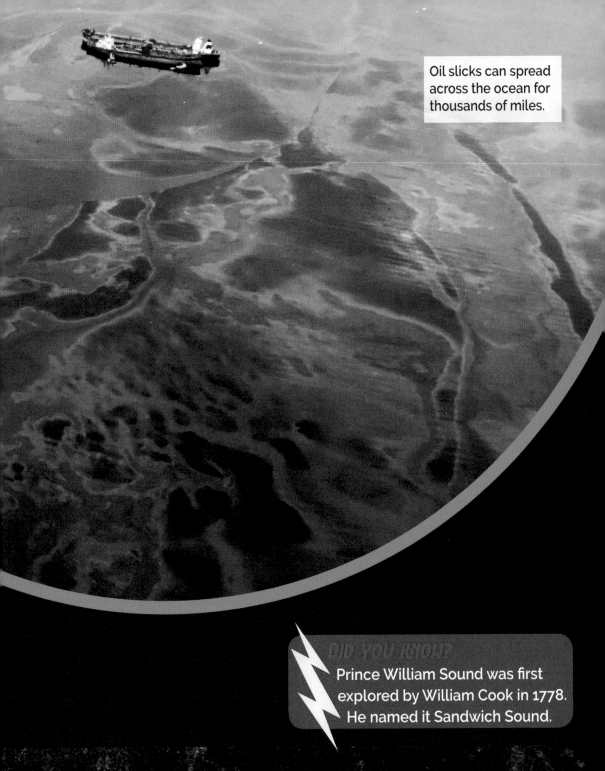

Oil slicks can spread across the ocean for thousands of miles.

DID YOU KNOW?
Prince William Sound was first explored by William Cook in 1778. He named it Sandwich Sound.

How and Why

Accidents and disasters often have more than one cause. Many different things come together to cause events that can greatly impact the future. Take a moment to explore some of the things that led to the *Exxon Valdez* oil spill.

Shipping Lanes

The *Exxon Valdez* left the Valdez, Alaska, port around 9:30 p.m. By 10:50 it had entered Prince William Sound. Prince William Sound has two shipping lanes. One of them travels toward the port. The other travels away. Ships can leave their lane if there are icebergs in their way. However, they're supposed to return quickly. The *Exxon Valdez* left its lane. It never went back.

One Officer

The Exxon company has many rules. One of them says that two officers must always be on watch. There was only one officer on watch when the ship hit the reef.

A Small, Tired Crew

The ship did not have enough workers. The small crew had been working too much, and hadn't gotten enough sleep. The person steering the ship didn't steer correctly. He never brought the ship back into the shipping lane like he should have.

A Single-Hulled Ship

The *Exxon Valdez*, like other oil tankers, had a single hull. This means that there was only one layer separating the inside of the ship from the water. Because of this, it was easy to break. Now, all oil tankers have to have a double hull. Double hulls are two single hulls on top of each other. If the outer one is broken, the ship still won't leak.

What Happened Next

As soon as the ship hit the reef, oil started to spill. It was enough to fill 17 Olympic-sized swimming pools. Animals began dying immediately. The chemicals in the oil poisoned seabirds, otters, and fish eggs. The oil also destroyed the animals' homes.

News outlets started reporting on the spill. They published pictures of the crash and the dying animals. People all over the world heard about it. The United States was very upset. Many people considered Alaska to be one of the last truly wild places in the country. Now its shore was covered in greasy, black oil.

People tried to figure out how to clean up the oil. The Exxon company, the state of Alaska, and the US response teams didn't know how to clean up a spill that large. By trying to clean it up, they could cause even more damage. Some beaches were washed in hot water. But this killed the **microorganisms** living there. The oil on the beaches went back into the ocean. The cleanup crews didn't take the oil out of the water. They just put it back in.

microorganism: a very small living thing which can only be seen using a microscope

Exxon spent billions of dollars trying to clean up the oil. Thousands of people were involved.

The *Exxon Valdez* was 987 feet (300 meters) long. It was carrying about 53 million gallons (200 million liters) of oil.

Ripple Effects

A single event, no matter how big or small it may seem at the time, can have a big impact on the future. The *Exxon Valdez* oil spill had many far-reaching effects.

Cleaning Up

The oil from the *Exxon Valdez* spill was difficult and dangerious to reach. Response teams couldn't clean up all the oil. People realized that they needed new ways to deal with oil spills. Many groups began to research how to clean up oil.

Many Spills

After the *Exxon Valdez* spill, there were many other oil spills around the United States. People began to realize that oil spills could be very dangerous. In August 1990, the Oil Pollution Act created many new oil laws. Today, ships that carry oil have to be stronger. Companies need to have plans to clean up any spills that happen.

Safe Food

The rest of the US buys a lot of fish from Alaska. After the *Exxon Valdez* oil spill, people all over the country began to worry that their food was poisoned. Scientists tested the wildlife for years to see if it was safe to eat. Those tests are still going on today.

Lost Money

The oil destroyed fishes' homes. People couldn't sell fish. Alaska lost millions of dollars. Tourism is also important in Alaska. Prince William Sound was a popular tourist spot. After the oil spill, the water was dirty and unsafe. People didn't want to visit anymore.

DID YOU KNOW?

In 2014, it was concluded that the sea otter population has almost completely recovered from the Exxon spill.

More than 99 percent of oil tankers arrive at their destinations without any problems. But the ones that do spill oil do lots of damage.

DEEPWATER HORIZON

On April 20, 2010, there was an explosion on an oil platform in the Gulf of Mexico. The platform was called *Deepwater Horizon*. Eleven workers were killed in the explosion. Seventeen more were injured. Oil began to pour out of the well into the ocean. The oil slick covered thousands of square miles. More than 200 million gallons (760 million liters) of oil was spilled. The *Deepwater Horizon* spill was the largest accidental oil spill in the world. In 2016, a movie was made about this tragedy.

The Legacy of Tragedy

The *Exxon Valdez* oil spill was one of the most televised environmental disasters. People saw many powerful images. Oil-covered birds, seals, and whales lay dead. Workers in bright plastic suits stood on black beaches. Dark clouds of oil spread through blue waters.

The people were upset. They demanded that companies pay for damage done to the environment. Exxon paid $2.1 billion to clean up the *Valdez* spill.

But all of that money can't fix everything. The Exxon oil spill caused many problems for Alaska. Now it is dangerous to catch fish there. People worry about being poisoned by the oil in the water. Alaska didn't seem pure and untouched anymore. Tourism has suffered.

Alaska's environment is still struggling. Some types of animals are doing much better. Many others are still not doing well. There is still oil beneath the sand on some beaches. This oil continues to hurt the animals that live there. Scientists think that the area may never completely recover.

DID YOU KNOW?
The oil company BP paid $42 billion to clean up the 2010 *Deepwater Horizon* spill.

Quiz

1

How much money did the workers at the Triangle Shirtwaist Factory make an hour?

Answer: 15 cents

2

How many new laws were passed because of the Triangle factory fire?

Answer: More than 30

3

The *Hindenburg*'s tank was filled with what kind of gas?

Answer: Hydrogen

4

The *Hindenburg* was built in what country?

Answer: Germany

5

What is the area around Chernobyl called?

Answer: The Exclusion Zone

6

When did the Chernobyl Nuclear Power Plant close?

Answer: 2000

7

What was the largest accidental oil spill in the world?

Answer: The *Deepwater Horizon* spill

8

How many gallons of oil spilled after the *Exxon Valdez* crashed?

Answer: About 11 million gallons (42 million liters)

Glossary

absorbent: a material that is used to soak up something else

current: water that moves in one direction

debris: scattered pieces of waste

ecosystem: a specific environment and the animals and plants that live there

fleet: a group of ships traveling together

hull: the body of a ship

immigrant: someone who moves to a new country

microorganism: a very small living thing which can only be seen using a microscope

mooring: a place where a boat or ship is tied up

morgue: a place where bodies are kept until they are identified and buried

newsreel: a short video about news or current affairs

radiation: a by-product of nuclear reactions; it is too small to be seen, but is very dangerous

reactor: the part of a nuclear power plant where nuclear reactions happen

reform: to make changes so that something is better

shirtwaist: a type of button-down shirt for women, popular in the early 1900s

union: a group of workers who work to protect their rights in the workplace

Index

Read More

Hopkinson, Deborah. *Hear My Sorrow: The Diary of Angela Denoto, a Shirtwaist Worker*. Dear America. New York, NY: Scholastic, 2004.

Otfinoski, Steven. *The Triangle Shirtwaist Factory Fire: Core Events of an Industrial Disaster*. North Mankato, MN: Capstone Press, 2014.

Rissman, Rebecca. *The Chernobyl Disaster*. Minneapolis, MN: ABDO Publishing Company, 2014.

Johnson, Rebecca L. *Chernobyl's Wild Kingdom: Life in the Dead Zone*. Minneapolis, MN: Lerner Publishing, 2015.

Pascal, Janet B., and David Groff. *What Was the Hindenburg?* New York, NY: Grosset & Dunlap, 2014.

Tarshis, Lauren. *I Survived the Hindenburg Disaster, 1937*. I survived. New York, NY: Scholastic, 2016.

Greeley, August. *Sludge And Slime: Oil Spills In Our World*. Man-Made Disasters. New York, NY: Rosen Publishing, 2003.

Gay, Kathlyn and Nigel Blundell. *The World's Worst Mistakes*. Making Headlines. New York NY: Enslow Publishing, 2017.